The Issachar A  book. It couldn[...] than this, when the people of God need to p[ossess the] reign as ordained by our Father. This book will enlighten your vision and empower your steps. Every Christian needs it!
—Josephine D. Ami-Narh, Leadership Expert and Head of HR Operations Office, Bank of Ghana

Real change will only come to those whose passion is great enough to make them question the questions that are being asked. In this book Apostle Akufo brings to light how to serve one's generation and achieve significance by questioning the status quo. It will help you break your "Jabez Box" of limitation.
—Apostle Dr. Aaron Ami-Narh, Senior Pastor, The Apostolic Church, Tema C5

Dr. Akufo, what an AWESOME book! Well written for this generation that has been searching for answers about THE WILL OF GOD for their lives to go to the next level. This book will bring insight and revelation to many who do not understand that their lives are full of different seasons according to the timing of God. It is a great tool in the hands of anyone who desires to be a WORLD CHANGER.
—Rev. Josephine Bessman, Co-director, Freetown Bible Training Center and Founder, Altar Builders Of Prayer Ministry (ABOP) Sierra Leone

THE ISSACHAR ANOINTING

Understanding Times
and Seasons
to Leverage Change

Kwabena Dautey Akufo

WESTBOW
PRESS®
A DIVISION OF THOMAS NELSON
& ZONDERVAN

Copyright © 2016 Kwabena Dautey Akufo.

All rights reserved. No part of this book may be used or reproduced by any means, graphic, electronic, or mechanical, including photocopying, recording, taping or by any information storage retrieval system without the written permission of the author except in the case of brief quotations embodied in critical articles and reviews.

Scriptures taken from the Holy Bible, New International Version®, NIV®. Copyright © 1973, 1978, 1984, 2011 by Biblica, Inc.™ Used by permission of Zondervan. All rights reserved worldwide. www.zondervan.com The "NIV" and "New International Version" are trademarks registered in the United States Patent and Trademark Office by Biblica, Inc.™ All rights reserved.

WestBow Press books may be ordered through booksellers or by contacting:

WestBow Press
A Division of Thomas Nelson & Zondervan
1663 Liberty Drive
Bloomington, IN 47403
www.westbowpress.com
1 (866) 928-1240

Because of the dynamic nature of the Internet, any web addresses or links contained in this book may have changed since publication and may no longer be valid. The views expressed in this work are solely those of the author and do not necessarily reflect the views of the publisher, and the publisher hereby disclaims any responsibility for them.

Any people depicted in stock imagery provided by Thinkstock are models, and such images are being used for illustrative purposes only. Certain stock imagery © Thinkstock.

ISBN: 978-1-5127-5667-8 (sc)
ISBN: 978-1-5127-5668-5 (e)

Library of Congress Control Number: 2016915137

Print information available on the last page.

WestBow Press rev. date: 09/09/2016

Contents

Preface		ix
1	Issachar Anointing for Understanding the Times	1
2	Issachar Anointing Qualities	12
3	Issachar Anointing Principles	23
4	Acquiring Issachar Anointing through the Holy Spirit	32
5	Acquiring Issachar Anointing through Spiritual Formation	50
6	Leveraging the Issachar Anointing to Change the Times and Seasons	57
7	Bible Study	75
Notes		79

Men of Issachar ... understood the times
and knew what Israel should do.

—1 Chronicles 12:32

[God] changes times and seasons; he sets up
kings and deposes them. He gives wisdom to
the wise and knowledge to the discerning.

—Daniel 2:21

Page Dedicated to APOSA * Arise and Build

Preface

This book is meant to help you to develop spiritually. It is not meant to increase your knowledge, though it will. It is meant for spiritual formation. I encourage you to read it prayerfully and practice the principles that you learn. Doing the Bible study at the end of the book will deepen your understanding. You may also use this book in a group Bible study.

I thank the Almighty God for grace in enabling me to write this book. His providence has been at work, because I didn't plan nor set out to write a book on this topic. Rather I was asked to be the keynote speaker at the APOSA (Apostolic Students and Associates) camp meeting held at Kwame Nkrumah University of Science and Technology (KNUST) in Ghana from December 26, 2015, through December 30, 2015. The theme assigned to me to treat in three main talks was "Understanding the Times and Seasons." Research for this topic led me to the Issachar Anointing concept.

Following the presentations, various people urged me to put the material into writing to benefit the larger Christian community. This was confirmation to me that I should endeavor to produce a book. I had been feeling, in the period leading up to the presentations, that the material I had developed was worth publishing.

I want to, therefore, thank the central executive committee of APOSA, led by Rev. Andy Nortey, for giving me the platform to produce this work. I also want to thank Apostle Dr. Aaron Ami-Narh and Lady Josephine Ami-Narh, who gave me exposure in the church community in Ghana that has resulted in many speaking opportunities, including the APOSA camp meeting talks. They were also the first to review an earlier draft of this manuscript, when it was only in teaching notes format. May God richly bless them and their descendants for promoting my ministry work in the Apostolic Church.

My wife was my greatest cheerleader, encouraging me to take the urgings of others to turn the teachings into a manuscript. She painstakingly reviewed the manuscript. As always, she has been an indispensable spiritual partner. I thank her for believing in my work. I honor my children, Teiko, Padikuor, and Dautey, who continue to endure my teachings since they have no choice!

All my achievements, including this book, are facilitated by God alone, to whom be honor, glory, majesty, power and authority, through Jesus Christ our Lord, before all ages, now and forevermore! Amen!

Kwabena Dautey Akufo
Andover, Massachusetts
July 2016

1

Issachar Anointing for Understanding the Times

Importance of Understanding the Times

There are many writings on the topic of "understanding the times," but most of them interpret the events and issues of a particular time period. There isn't much that I can add by doing the same thing about our current times.

I believe what will be helpful is to present a framework that you can use to understand the times in your personal life, family, church, community, nation, and the world. This will enable you to develop a response to your understanding of the times. May God help me to do so! Let me explain with this illustration.

If I asked you what the time is, you would look at your watch or phone and tell me the time. If you had an analog watch like mine, you might not know how to tell the time. In the past, when people didn't know how to tell the time, they lied and said that their watch had stopped working or that they needed eyeglasses to see the time.

If I don't possess a watch or don't know how to tell the time, I'll always have to ask someone else for the time. I will have to rely on that person's accuracy and trustworthiness in reading the time. If, however, I learn how to tell the time for myself, then I won't have to ask anymore.

Furthermore, when I ask for the time, it is for a purpose. I may be trying to find out how much time I have left to finish a task, whether it is time for me to do something, or whether I am running late for an event. Once I know what the time is, I can act on that information. Consequently, I need to be confident that the time is a reliable reading, because actions important to me are dependent on it. If I don't know what the time is, I will not be able to react to the time. My actions, if any, in that case may just be force of habit.

In the same way, if you know how to determine the times you're in, then you'll know what to do about it—and then do it. Those who are able to understand the times and seasons can act to take advantage of emerging times and seasons. Those who are able to understand the times and seasons influence their generations in unimaginable ways.

It is therefore important to equip yourself to understand the times and seasons so that you can influence your generation, your community, your nation, and your world. The set of qualities that will enable you to accomplish this goal is what I call the *Issachar Anointing*. The Issachar Anointing is named after the men of Issachar, who the Bible tells us were uniquely qualified to understand the times and seasons and direct Israel how to act.

The Issachar Anointing

Effects of Understanding the Times, Even in the Secular World

An expert surfer has the skill to sense when a big wave is rising, and then to position himself or herself to ride the big wave successfully. Expert surfers acquire this skill by learning the fundamentals of surfing and how to sense an oncoming big wave.

In the same way, when you are equipped to sense the emerging times and seasons, you can act accordingly, to your benefit and to the benefit of your generation.

At the turn of the twentieth century, the automobile was manufactured for use by the very wealthy only. Specially trained people were required to drive the owner around—that is, a car was a specialty machine that needed a pilot, like an airplane is today. The masses used horse-drawn carriages.

Henry Ford entered this situation and saw an emerging trend—replacement of horse-drawn carriages by the automobile. He declared, "I will build a motor car for the great multitude."[1] He could foresee cars completely replacing horse-drawn carriages. Through dint of hard work, the first automobile for the common person was born a year later in 1908. When Henry Ford understood the times, he acted accordingly and influenced not only his generation but also future generations. Yesterday when you sat in a car, you might not have remembered the origins of the automobile. From now on when you sit in a car, remember that you're benefiting because Henry Ford understood the times and responded with generation-influencing actions.

In the 1970s, a computer occupied a complete room and was operated by people trained in computer science. By 1980, the common computer in use was the minicomputer, which was about the size of a sport utility vehicle. Computers were owned and operated only by medium to large companies.

Then in 1980, Bill Lowe at IBM proposed to build a computer that could be used by the ordinary person rather than by computer experts. IBM was so bureaucratic and institutionalized that it was not possible to build this kind of computer within the standard operations of the company. Lowe convinced the bureaucracy to let him do things differently, and they agreed because the potential financial loss if he failed was small.

Bill Lowe led a small team that outsourced the processor to Intel and the operating system to an unknown firm called Microsoft; other key components were outsourced to other outside firms. By 1981, the personal computer (PC) was born. The PC was the precursor of all of today's personal computing devices, such as laptop computers, tablets, and smartphones. Lowe understood the times—he could see the future, and when he put together the past, present, and future, he saw the big picture. When he understood the times, he acted accordingly and influenced his own and future generations.

When you understand the times, then you are able to act accordingly to influence your generation, just as Henry Ford and Bill Lowe did.

Issachar Anointing Promotes Understanding of the Times

Consider the following text from 1 Chronicles:

> These are the numbers of the men armed for battle who came to David at Hebron to turn Saul's kingdom over to him, as the LORD had said: men of Judah, carrying shield and spear—6,800 armed for battle; men of Simeon, warriors ready for battle—7,100;
>
> men of Levi—4,600, including Jehoiada, leader of the family of Aaron, with 3,700 men, and Zadok, a brave young warrior, with 22 officers from his family;
>
> men of Benjamin, Saul's kinsmen—3,000, most of whom had remained loyal to Saul's house until then;
>
> men of Ephraim, brave warriors, famous in their own clans—20,800;
>
> men of half the tribe of Manasseh, designated by name to come and make David king—18,000;
>
> men of Issachar, who understood the times and knew what Israel should do—200 chiefs, with all their relatives under their command;
>
> men of Zebulun, experienced soldiers prepared for battle with every type of

weapon, to help David with undivided loyalty—50,000;

men of Naphtali—1,000 officers, together with 37,000 men carrying shields and spears;

men of Dan, ready for battle—28,600;

men of Asher, experienced soldiers prepared for battle—40,000;

and from east of the Jordan, men of Reuben, Gad and the half-tribe of Manasseh, armed with every type of weapon—120,000.

All these were fighting men who volunteered to serve in the ranks. They came to Hebron fully determined to make David king over all Israel. All the rest of the Israelites were also of one mind to make David king. (12:23-38)

Verse 32 of this text says, "men of Issachar, who understood the times and knew what Israel should do—200 chiefs, with all their relatives under their command." So, of all the tribes of Israel, the men of Issachar uniquely understood the times and acted accordingly. They influenced their generation by promoting the greatest dynasty physically and spiritually: the Davidic dynasty forever perpetuated by the kingship of Jesus Christ.

The set of qualities that enabled the men of Issachar to understand the times and take action is what I call the Issachar Anointing. May you acquire the Issachar

Anointing to understand the times and seasons of your life to enable you to influence your generation!

Definition of Times and Seasons

God interrupts the pattern of events to effect paradigmatic changes that mark periods as stated in Daniel 2:21: "He changes times and seasons; he sets up kings and deposes them. He gives wisdom to the wise and knowledge to the discerning."

The times are the thinking, worldviews, occurrences, and situations that characterize a time period in a given location, and sociocultural or religious grouping. You can have the times in the world, in a nation, in a church, in an organization, or in a community. For example, in the political arena, the world is currently in the times of terrorism. It is simultaneously in the times of globalization as a socioeconomic phenomenon. It recently went through the times of the Cold War.

In these times of terrorism, thinking centers on religious tension, sociocultural imperialism, terrorism prevention, and more. A primary worldview is that the terrorism narrative governs conflicts, uprisings, and criminal activity. Occurrences in the times of terrorism include the 9/11 attacks on the World Trade Center in New York City; the 2004 Madrid bombings; the 7/7 London bombings in 2005; the 2015 Paris massacres; the Bamako, Mali hotel attacks in 2015; the Burkina Faso hotel attacks in 2016; the Brussels airport attack in 2016; and many more. Situations characterizing the times of terrorism include heightened airport security, expensive plane tickets due to security surcharges, invasion of privacy by security agencies, and many others.

When new times emerge, systems and structures that supported the old times are removed and new ones are established. Consequently, there is a new order (structure, system, practice, and government), new worldview, new modus operandi (a way of doing things), and a paradigm shift (change in understanding of how things work).

Lily Rothman wrote that "The Annals of the centuries are nothing more than individual days sewn together, and those who keep the records use their own needle and thread."[2] Understanding the times is a review of the past, present, and future. It consists of taking the days of the past and present and the expected days of the future and sewing them together to produce a quilt of days. Then you take a view of the quilt as a whole to understand its patterns and color scheme, giving you a composite picture of the times.

The men of Issachar, we will see later, had the unique gift to construct such a composite picture to understand the times and then act accordingly. This special gift is what I call the Issachar Anointing.

May God give you the Issachar Anointing to see the composite picture of the times, understand the times, and act accordingly to impact your generation!

Seasons are like times in definition, but are components of times. That is, there are seasons within times. A season is characterized by the general conditions governing your life or an organization's life in a given location.

For example, within the times of the incarnation, there was a season of John the Baptist's ministry, followed by the season of Jesus's ministry, followed by the season of the apostles' ministry. Just as one has to discern the times, so also one has to discern the seasons. John the Baptist's disciples had to transition from the season of repentance baptism into the season of Holy Spirit baptism.

Unique Anointing of Men of Issachar Enabled Them to Lead Israel in David's Coronation

The 1 Chronicles passage quoted above lists Israel's delegation to enthrone David. David had ruled in Hebron for seven and a half years, over only the tribe of Judah (2 Sam. 2:11), while Ishbosheth, Saul's son, ruled over the remainder of Israel (2 Sam. 2:8-10). Abner, the commander of Israel's army who had established and sustained Ishbosheth's kingship, was murdered, and it created a power vacuum and weakness in Israel. In the context of this power vacuum, Ishbosheth was murdered by two leaders of raiding bands, known today in America as special forces. Consequently, the tribes decided to come under David's kingship. Delegations were sent from each tribe, as listed in the passage, to make David king over all of Israel.

They wanted David to be king

How did all Israel decide to make David king after the death of Ishbosheth?

Verse 23 introduces the passage: "These are the numbers of the men armed for battle who came to David at Hebron to turn Saul's kingdom over to him, as the Lord had said." Verse 38 concludes the passage by restating that purpose, saying, "All these were fighting men who volunteered to serve in the ranks. They came to Hebron fully determined to make David king over all Israel." So, unquestionably, the military representatives had the goal to effect a smooth transition of power from Saul's dynasty to David's dynasty—a transition from one era to another, a transition from civil war to peace, a transition from unordained kingship to ordained kingship.

The passage lists the numerical strength of the militaries of each of the twelve tribes of Israel, "who came to David at Hebron to turn Saul's kingdom over to him." In some listings, the author gives a commentary about the men's quality that was relevant for the coronation of David, such as their military expertise or loyalty. About halfway through the list, the author comments not on the expertise but on the character of the men of Issachar, saying that they "understood the times and knew what Israel should do."

It is odd that in this statistical listing that only the men of Issachar were singled out for such a comment. The commentary on the men of Issachar was unique because they possessed unique qualities, which I call the Issachar Anointing.

It is clear that the men of Issachar influenced the nation to choose to make David king, based on their understanding and knowledge.

May God grant you unique qualities of the Issachar Anointing to impact your generation!

2

Issachar Anointing Qualities

We know that Issachar was the ninth child of Jacob and spawned the tribe called Issachar. There isn't much about Issachar in the Bible, but we can develop a set of qualities of his tribe from the Bible and extrabiblical sources.

In ancient times, there were religious books, known today as extrabiblical sources, which were written as commentaries on the Bible, similar to the way religious books are written today. Such books provide insights into the events that took place during Bible times and also give interpretations of the Bible. Two such well-respected extrabiblical sources are the Midrash and the Targum. The Midrash is a commentary written by rabbinical sages from the post-temple era (immediately after AD 70). It contains exegesis of the Torah and homiletic (sermon) stories that expand upon gaps in the Torah. The Targum is a collection of Aramaic translations or paraphrases of the Old Testament.

Intellectual Excellence, Biblical Scholarship, and Legal Expertise

Issachar Anointing includes intellectual excellence, biblical scholarship, and legal expertise.

Numbers 7:18 shows that the leader of Issachar was the second after Judah to bring his offering after the altar built by Moses was anointed, even though Issachar was the ninth son born of Jacob. It is believed that the Issachar leader presented second because the tribe of Issachar were considered as experts of the Law.[1]

According to the ancient Jewish religious book called the Midrash, the men of Issachar were skilled at Jewish evangelism, equaled the Levites in biblical scholarship, and represented "the pattern of learning."[2] The men of Issachar gained intellectual excellence, biblical scholarship, and legal expertise through much study of Scripture and other religious books.

In the same way, if you spend much time studying the Bible and other theologically sound religious books under the guidance of the Holy Spirit, you will become an expert in knowing the Word, knowing the ways of God, and knowing how to apply the Word of God to any situation.

May you voraciously study the Word of God to gain Issachar Anointing in the form of spiritual knowledge and intellectual capability!

Expertise in Astronomy and Astrological Interpretations

Issachar Anointing also includes insight into revelations and into astronomical and astrological events.

"According to the Targum, [the men of Issachar understanding the times and knowing what Israel ought to do] meant that they knew how to ascertain the periods of the sun and moon, the intercalation of months, the dates of solemn feasts, and could interpret the signs of the times."[3] This means the men of Issachar had expertise in interpreting revelations and astronomical and astrological events. This skill most likely was Yahweh inspired, just as the magi from the East followed the unique star to Jerusalem to look for the newborn Messiah.

Such spiritual inspiration can only come if you spend time waiting upon the Lord in prayer and meditation, and seeking to hear from God. We know Daniel received much spiritual inspiration because of his habit of waiting upon the Lord. If you spend time waiting upon the Lord in prayer and fasting, God will give you insight into revelations, signs, and events in your community, the nation, the world, and the universe.

May you spend quality time waiting upon God to gain Issachar Anointing to receive uncommon revelations and spiritual signs!

Wisdom and Prophetic Insight

Issachar Anointing includes wisdom and prophetic insight. Consider Numbers 7:1–3:

> When Moses finished setting up the tabernacle, he anointed it and consecrated it and all its furnishings. He also anointed and consecrated the altar and all its utensils. Then the leaders of Israel, the heads of families who were the tribal leaders in charge of those who were counted, made offerings. They brought as their gifts before the LORD six covered carts and twelve oxen—an ox from each leader and a cart from every two. These they presented before the tabernacle.

According to the Midrash, it is the tribe of Issachar who suggested this donation—a reflection of their wisdom.[4]

Also according to the Midrash, the seven wise men of Persia and Media consulted by King Xerxes of Persia when his queen, Vashti, refused to display her beauty for his royal guests were men of Issachar.[5] In fact Esther 1:13 speaks of them as "men who understood the times," which connects with our key verse in 1 Chronicles 12:32.

As I said earlier, in the listing of delegates from each tribe for David's coronation, the necessary qualities were emphasized. Military strength was the main quality of almost all the tribes except for Issachar, whose military expertise was completely omitted. The quality that was important about Issachar was their wisdom and prophetic insight.

Understanding as high-level aggregation of data

The fundamental basis for wisdom is understanding. Understanding results from a process that begins with data acquisition and leads to its intelligent and supernatural aggregation, ultimately resulting in understanding.

Gene Bellinger and his colleagues wrote an article called "Data, Information, Knowledge, and Wisdom," in which they show that data is systematically aggregated into understanding to form the basis for wisdom.[6] In this section, I give a simplified synopsis of their article, using some clarifying examples.

Data is raw information or uninterpreted fact. For example, the statements "It is raining" and "There are no drains" are data, or facts that have not been interpreted.

Information is created when a connection between data is established and/or when the data is interpreted. For example, the statement "The clouds darkened and then it started raining" takes two pieces of data and connects them interpretatively, providing more insight into the thought being conveyed.

Knowledge is the application of data and/or information. It is a deduction of general patterns, principles, and procedures. Consider this knowledge statement: "When cumulus clouds form and the humidity is high, it is likely to rain." This is a generalization from the information that says, "The clouds darkened and then it started raining," integrated with data that says, "Dark clouds are cumulus clouds," and information that says, "High humidity is a precursor to rain." This generalization describes how rain is formed in a particular area.

Here is another knowledge statement: "When there is no drainage, rain can cause flooding."

Understanding takes place when you develop new knowledge from existing sets of knowledge. Consider the statement, "In an area where cumulus clouds frequently form and humidity is often high and the drainage is poor, there is likely to be frequent flooding." This takes the two pieces of knowledge from our previous examples and intelligently connects them to provide new knowledge as to why flooding is frequent in an area. The resulting knowledge is deeper than the unconnected pieces. It enables you to deduce what is going on.

Understanding can be deductive, intuitive, or supernatural. When understanding is intuitive or supernatural, it becomes discernment.

Wisdom as evaluated understanding

Wisdom is the application of the results of understanding. For example, when you understand that heavy and frequent rainfall in poor drainage areas can cause floods, then that understanding factors into the decision as to whether to build a drainage system. The process of going from this understanding of flooding to a decision to build a comprehensive drainage system is wisdom. So, we can say that wisdom is discerning and making right choices. Knowing the right choice but failing to make it is not wisdom.

Worldview is one of the factors influencing your understanding. A biblical worldview means that the intelligence you apply to aggregate data into understanding is influenced by biblical principles. True wisdom cannot be devoid of biblical principles.

Therefore, we can modify the definition of wisdom by saying that wisdom is discerning and then making right and godly choices.

There are many misconceptions about what constitutes wisdom and how it manifests itself. Wisdom is not general knowledge. The illiterate man may exercise more wisdom than the well-read traveler. Wisdom is not academic knowledge. The open-air market trader may exercise more wisdom than the PhD. Wisdom is not biblical knowledge. The unschooled Christian may exercise more wisdom than the theologian. Wisdom is not learned by observing and experiencing life, as Eliphaz thought (Job 4:7–8, 5:3, 27). They just contribute to wisdom. Wisdom is not inherited from the past, as Bildad thought (Job 8:8–9, 18:5–21). Wisdom does not belong to those the world considers wise, as Zophar thought (Job 11:6, 20:1–29). Wisdom is not common sense. Common sense is the result of wisdom.

Wisdom is a quality of the Issachar Anointing

The statement that the men of Issachar "understood the times" means that they had deductive, intuitive, and supernatural understanding. They discerned the situation correctly, and hence they "knew what Israel should do," which means they directed Israel to act upon that discernment. Diagnosis must lead to prescription. This is the essence of wisdom as we have defined it. So the men of Issachar understood the times because they had wisdom as an element of their anointing.

The English translation of the Septuagint (itself a translation of the Old Testament from Hebrew into Greek) renders our key text as follows: "And of the sons of Issachar having wisdom with regard to the times, knowing what Israel should do, two hundred; and all their brethren with them" (1 Chron. 12:32). The quality described as "wisdom with regard to the times" is part of the Issachar Anointing. When you acquire the Issachar Anointing, you get wisdom.

Wisdom and prophetic insight belong to God. He is the only one who gives it out. Just as Solomon asked God for wisdom, so also you must ask God to give you wisdom to enable you to understand the times. Similarly, God is the source and interpreter of prophecy. You must ask God for prophetic insight into any situation. This requires much prayer time before God, in meditation and submission to his purposes.

May God grant you wisdom and prophetic insight of the Issachar Anointing!

Astute Leadership and Strategic Thinking and Planning

The Issachar Anointing also includes astute leadership skills and strategic thinking and planning skills.

Except for Issachar, all other tribes had thousands of soldiers listed. Issachar had only two hundred chiefs listed. Granted, their relatives were under them, but the Bible does not state their numbers. This means the writer wants us to take notice of the paltry two hundred in comparison to the thousands from other tribes. The author wants us to also notice the fact that the men of Issachar were not ordinary men, but chiefs. While the other tribes were armed for war, the men of Issachar were armed with the qualities described as understanding of the times and knowledge of what should be done in response to the times. This tells us that understanding the times and acting accordingly are as powerful as a huge military. This is another reason why the Issachar Anointing is an important quality to possess.

Among the other tribes, some were distinguished as "leaders" or "officers." The word translated from the Hebrew into "leader" has the connotation of a person occupying the front, as in leading people into battle. On the other hand, the word translated from the Hebrew into "chief" has the connotation of a "head," who is on top. Issachar's two hundred chiefs were hierarchically on top, and hence were in a strategic position. They provided strategic thinking and planning.

The Issachar Anointing

When you're standing on top of a mountain, you can see clearly what is going on in the valley below. When you're leading a group in the valley, you can't see the entire picture of what's going on. Issachar's chiefs, because they were on top and not in front, were therefore strategically placed to see the big picture and develop suitable plans to deal with it.

In the book of Judges, Deborah, a woman, arose as president and led Israel into war against Canaan, with Barak as her military commander. Only a few of the tribes supported the campaign, including the tribe of Issachar. In listing the tribes who supported the campaign, Deborah made reference to "princes of Issachar": "The princes of Issachar were with Deborah; yes, Issachar was with Barak, rushing after him into the valley" (Judg. 5:15). Note that the princes of Issachar were with Deborah, the person in command, while the rest of the tribe was with Barak at the front. In fact, the only group that was with Deborah were the princes of Issachar. They served as presidential advisers, astute leaders, and cabinet members. This further reinforces their role as strategic thinkers and planners. Consider also that the Hebrew word translated into "prince" is a slight variation on the word translated into "chief," and also has the connotation of being the head and on top.

The men of Issachar were astute leaders, equipped with strategic thinking skills and strategic planning skills. God endows people with such leadership skills. Leadership[7] and administration[8] are each gifts of the Holy Spirit. To acquire the leadership skills of strategic thinking and planning in the Issachar Anointing, you must subdue yourself so that the Holy Spirit may operate these gifts through you.

May God grant you the Holy Spirit gifts of leadership and administration and equip you with strategic thinking and planning skills of the Issachar Anointing!

Summary

The unique anointing of the men of Issachar enabled them to understand the times and to then influence and lead Israel to make David king. I call this anointing the Issachar Anointing, which includes the following qualities:

- intellectual excellence, biblical scholarship, and legal expertise;
- expertise in astronomy and astrological interpretations;
- wisdom and prophetic insight; and
- astute leadership and strategic thinking/planning.

3

Issachar Anointing Principles

Here are five principles that are inherent in the Issachar Anointing. I believe if you apply them, they will help you understand the times.

Seek Biblical Insights into Situations or Events

The first Issachar Anointing principle for understanding the times is to seek biblical insights into situations or events. As I said earlier, the men of Issachar were students of Scripture and studied it voraciously. Their scriptural learning was equal to that of the Levites. This gave them scriptural insights into situations and events. To apply the Issachar Anointing principles for understanding the times, you need to know the Bible very well.

After fifty years of Judah's exile in Babylon, Daniel understood that the times were about to change. He had learned that Jeremiah prophesied seventy years of captivity. Daniel said, "In the first year of his reign, I, Daniel, understood from the Scriptures, according to the word of the LORD given to Jeremiah the prophet [Jeremiah 29:10], that the desolation of Jerusalem would last seventy years. So I turned to the Lord God and pleaded with him in prayer and petition, in fasting, and in sackcloth and ashes" (Dan. 9:2–3). To confirm his understanding of Scripture, he turned to God in prayer and fasting. Then he got revelation to confirm his scriptural understanding.

We've seen incredible wickedness, of a type our generation has never experienced, in the ISIS military campaigns. The world sees ISIS as another terrorist organization. But perhaps there is more to their arrival on the world scene than meets the eye. Such innovative wickedness may have biblical underpinnings, as we read in Romans 1:28–32. To confirm this, you will need to wait upon the Lord in prayer and fasting. Then God will reveal to you how this new world phenomenon connects with the Bible and how you must handle it.

May God give you biblical insights into situations and events in your life!

Be Observant, Study Abnormal Events, and Ask God for Further Illumination

The second Issachar Anointing principle for understanding the times is to be observant, study abnormal events, and ask God for further illumination. God sometimes gives signs through abnormal events.

When Jesus was crucified, the world went dark for three hours. Some failed to see its significance. If they had sought illumination from God, they would have discovered that the times of grace had been ushered in by the crucifixion of our Lord Jesus Christ.

A book called Leadership on the Line uses the illustration of going to the balcony in a dance hall in order to see the entire dance floor.[1] This allows you to see better what is happening on the dance floor, such as who is dancing with whom, how certain people are dancing together, what type of dance each pair is doing, and so on. If you're on the dance floor, you cannot see the dynamics of the dancers as well.

This means in order to understand the times, you need to step back periodically. Go to the balcony and look at the big picture of life in order to get the larger perspective. Then wait upon the Lord in fasting and prayer for insight into the observations you have made.

The world has been experiencing worsening natural disasters and more intense weather events. In the year 2015, Hurricane Patricia became the most intense tropical cyclone on record, with winds of two hundred miles per hour. Flooding has become rampant worldwide. The unusual combination of fire within floodwaters that killed many people in Accra, Ghana, in 2015 is ominous. Romans 8:20–22 may give some clues as to the meaning of these events. Ask God in prayer and fasting.

May God illuminate your observations of abnormal events!

Challenge Prevailing Assumptions, Ideas, and Wisdom

The third Issachar Anointing principle for understanding the times is to challenge prevailing assumptions, ideas, and wisdom. I believe the men of Issachar were not in favor of Ishbosheth being the king instead of David, but it took them some time to convince the rest of the tribes. They did not accept the prevailing assumption that the heir to the throne should be Saul's son.

One way of challenging the prevailing assumptions, ideas, and wisdom is to question the common questions that people ask. Change the questions to get new insights. Through socialization, we have come to certain understandings about our world. When we are daring enough, we push the boundaries of those understandings by asking questions. But the questions we ask are limited by those same understandings. The answer you get to a question may be correct in relation to the question, but not necessarily right within the world of understandings, including both your understanding and others' understanding. That is why it is necessary sometimes to explore whether the question is even right to begin with.

Here is an example: an elder came to visit us, and my wife asked him whether he would like to eat *kenkey* or *banku*. (Each is a corn-based Ghanaian meal.) The question seemed appropriate within the understanding of my wife and the understanding of the elder. But within the larger space of understanding, this question limited the scope of the answer to two: kenkey or banku.

Since I knew that the elder's favorite food was *fufu* (a plantain-based Ghanaian meal) with soup, I commented that the question needed to be changed. I asked the elder, "What type of food would you like to eat?"

When I questioned the original question and changed it, that act opened up the set of possible foods to choose from. Fufu with soup became a possible answer. And my wife remembered that she had pepper chicken soup that she could use for that meal.

Institutions have the habit of limiting the questions asked in order not to rock the boat, because they have limited answers. They allow variations on the questions, but not transformational new questions that open up the set of possible answers and could take the institution in a different direction. The answer that you get to a question will cause you to act or keep you where you are. Since the question dictates the set of possible answers, it is in the interest of institutions to limit the questions to the ones that provide self-preserving answers. Such institutions run the risk of becoming irrelevant. On the other hand, organizations that allow transformational questions increase their chances of reinventing themselves to flow with emerging times.

People in general are uncomfortable about questioning their socialized understanding or allowing others to question it. They are only comfortable asking the same types of questions they've always asked. Some people in authority have failed miserably because they refused to accept new questions about their understanding. Consequently, they did not see the changes in the times that new questions would have exposed.

Bill Lowe questioned the socialized understanding that computers were meant for organizations in a central computer center, and not for individuals on their desktops. Because of his innovative questioning, IBM was able to reinvent itself and stay alive during the desktop PC era. Other major computer companies who focused on company-size computers went completely out of business.

King Rehoboam failed as king and lost control over the tribes because he did not accept questioning of the socialized understanding of massive taxes imposed for forty years by his father, King Solomon.

When Sir Isaac Newton discovered the law of gravity, the story has it that he was sitting under an apple tree. An apple fell down. He could have assumed the apple fell down because it was ripe. But he asked the groundbreaking question about what force pushed the apple down.

When you push yourself to ask or accept questions beyond your space of socialized understanding, you will begin to see new trends or paradigm shifts that may be part of changing times. You must question the questions that you've been asking in your church, your community, your organization, your society, and your nation. You must develop transformational new questions. This will help you to challenge prevailing assumptions, ideas, and wisdom.

Examine Biblical Foundations of Dogma and Embrace New Biblical Insights

The fourth Issachar Anointing principle for understanding the times is to examine biblical foundations of dogma, which are beliefs and traditions, and embrace new biblical insight.

The church runs by Scripture and tradition. Tradition may change from generation to generation and from location to location to deal with the specific situations of a given generation in a given location. Scripture never changes.

Jesus was fond of questioning traditions because they are not Scripture and must change as appropriate. In fact, his major run-ins with the Pharisees were over his questioning the biblical foundations of their traditions. In a sense he was asking transformational questions of their practices. Those who understood his questioning came to understand the emerging times of grace. Those who didn't eventually became irrelevant as they clung to dying traditions.

Consider the location of church services. In the months following Jesus' ascension, the church met in synagogues. In the first century AD, services were held in homes. In later centuries, services were held in special buildings. In twenty-first century China, many churches hold services in homes. If you don't understand the biblical foundations of church service location, you may be stuck in an old tradition and miss the changing times concerning church service locations.

Consider the Pentecostal revival in the early twentieth century. The church worldwide had come to accept the cessation of overt acts by the Holy Spirit. This meant that there was no Holy Spirit baptism with speaking in tongues, healing, deliverance, prophecies, miraculous works, and so on. The people used by God in the Pentecostal revival sought to reexamine this prevailing understanding of the overt acts of the Holy Spirit. They did this by examining scriptural teaching on the subject. They gained new biblical insight that enabled them to understand and flow with the times being ushered by God. They received the Holy Spirit baptism with speaking in tongues, and went on to exercise various gifts of the Holy Spirit, just as the churches in Acts had done. So the Pentecostal revival that has spread even to conservative denominations is partly the result of people examining the biblical foundations of dogma and embracing new biblical insight.

Examine biblical foundations of dogma and embrace new biblical insights to apply the Issachar Anointing principles.

Examine the Worldview Basis of Prevailing Thoughts and Principles

The fifth Issachar Anointing principle for understanding the times is to examine the worldview basis of prevailing thoughts and principles.

Former American president Jimmy Carter once said, "We must adjust to changing times and still hold to unchanging principles." Is the worldview underlying the principle biblical, idolatrous, or secular? Knowing this will help you decide whether to discard or adopt the principle. If a new principle is idolatrous, then you must avoid it.

In the early days of The Apostolic Church in Ghana, drums were prohibited at church services. It was believed they were instruments of Satan because they were also used for idolatrous purposes. A similar belief was held in the United States concerning the electric guitar. When you examine the worldview underlying these beliefs, it is devoid of biblical understanding. Such an examination allows you to understand and accept the new times in Christian music.

Examine the worldview underlying prevailing thoughts and principles. Be open to change those that are devoid of biblical worldview.

4

Acquiring Issachar Anointing through the Holy Spirit

The Holy Spirit Is at the Heart of the Issachar Anointing

Consider the following passage:

> However, as it is written: "No eye has seen, no ear has heard, no mind has conceived what God has prepared for those who love him"—but God has revealed it to us by his Spirit. The Spirit searches all things, even the deep things of God. For who among men knows the thoughts of a man except the man's spirit within him? In the same way no one knows the thoughts of God except the Spirit of God. (1 Cor. 2:9–11)

We learned earlier from Daniel 2:21 that God is the one who orchestrates the times. Therefore he is the one to uniquely reveal the times and seasons. From verses 9–10 of this passage, we can deduce that no one knows how God has orchestrated the times except for the Spirit of God. Verse 10 directly tells us that the Spirit of God knows all the deep things of God. This same Spirit of God reveals those deep things of God to those who have the Spirit of God!

Therefore, the Holy Spirit knows exactly what the times and seasons are or will be, and can reveal them to those who possess the Holy Spirit. This means that true believers, indwelt by the Holy Spirit and in tune with the Holy Spirit through daily infilling, can receive from the Holy Spirit revelation of the times and seasons.

The Holy Spirit is the agent for revealing the times and seasons to those who are alert to his promptings. Peter tells us how some prophets enlisted the indwelling Holy Spirit to discover the times of grace: "Concerning this salvation, the prophets, who spoke of the grace that was to come to you, searched intently and with the greatest care, trying to find out the time and circumstances to which the Spirit of Christ in them was pointing when he predicted the sufferings of Christ and the glories that would follow" (1 Pet. 1:10–11).

Because the Holy Spirit is the orchestrator and revealer of the times, we can deduce that the Holy Spirit is at the heart of the Issachar Anointing. So to acquire the Issachar Anointing, you need to seek the indwelling and daily infilling of the Holy Spirit.

The Holy Spirit-Powered Issachar Anointing Makes You an Ambassador of Heaven

An ambassador is accredited by his home country to represent its interests in a foreign country. The ambassador has a channel of communication with his home country, through which he receives information about his home country's plans with respect to the foreign country and also information on secret plans of the foreign country that the home country has discovered. The home country sends instructions to the ambassador as to what to do in regard to these plans.

Philippians 3:20 tells us that as a true believer, you are a citizen of heaven. Further, 2 Corinthians 5:20 says that as a believer, you are also an ambassador of heaven, resident in this world. It is the indwelling Holy Spirit that makes you a citizen and an ambassador.

The kingdom of heaven uses the Holy Spirit as the medium of communication to send you revelations of the plans of heaven regarding this world. That communication enables you as an ambassador to understand the times and seasons of the foreign country we call Earth. The Holy Spirit instructs you what to do on behalf of heaven in response to the times and seasons of Earth. This is what I have defined as the Issachar Anointing.

The Holy Spirit gives you the Issachar Anointing to be ambassador of heaven to this world, eligible to receive revelation of the times and seasons and revelation as to what to do in response to the times and seasons.

Through the Holy Spirit, Be Part of God's Orchestration of the Times

"The fullness of time" refers to the times or season

Consider Galatians 4:4-5: "But when the time had fully come, God sent his Son, born of a woman, born under law, to redeem those under law, that we might receive the full rights of sons."

This passage says, "When the time had fully come" and not "when the time had come." "When the time had come" means, for example, that you set a date for your wedding, and when that day arrived, you had the wedding whether things were ready or not.

This is not what the text says. The adjective "fully" qualifies the nature of the time being spoken of. So the text may be rendered as "in the fullness of time." That is, it is a time that is full.

The word "time" here, *kronos* in Greek, means also a period of time and not a point in time.

The word "fully" here, *pleroma* in Greek, comes from the context of preparing a ship for sailing. When the cargo and supplies have been loaded into the ship, the oarsmen and sailors have boarded, the guards have boarded, the passengers have boarded, and the sails have been mounted—then the captain boards and determines that the ship is seaworthy. Then the time is deemed to be full. The ship is ready to sail. Specific events and occurrences have reached fruition. They characterize what we've referred to as the times.

The fullness of time, therefore, means that certain systems, structures, practices, governments, worldviews, modus operandi, and paradigm shifts have become established. In other words, it is the dawn of new times or seasons. We can paraphrase this passage by saying that when the relevant times had arrived, "God sent his son, born of a woman, born under law," to inaugurate the times of grace.

God had to prepare the world for the dawn of the times of grace

When you are going to produce a movie, you get a script. You get actors who can act well. You get a set, props, set technicians, light technicians, and costumes. You get musicians, sound systems, and sound engineers. It takes months, sometimes years to put all of this together. And when everything is ready, then you can say, "Lights, camera, action." The time has fully come. The times are ripe.

Similarly, after the Adamic fall and God's establishment of the Adamic covenant, God had to prepare the world for the time to fully come to execute that covenant. God had to develop a script, actors, set, and so on. The story of the redemption act, which is the Old Testament, had to be in place. Then the actors had to be brought on the world stage.

Zechariah had to be born and become a priest to father John the Baptist. John had to engage in his ministry as the forerunner of Jesus to prepare the way

The Issachar Anointing

for Jesus. Mary had to come into existence, maintain her virginity as a young girl, and have a pure faith. Joseph had to engage her for marriage and be a godly man who accepted divine revelation, receptive to marrying the pregnant Mary. The angel Gabriel had to appear to Zechariah and then to Mary, to announce the dawn of a new era.

The script called for Christ to be crucified on a cross in the Roman manner, rather than stoned to death, as was done in Israel. Crucifixion had to become a practice in Israel, and so Rome had to become the governing power over Palestine. So the Roman Empire had to come into existence and absorb existing empires.

When all these actors were ready and the socioeconomic and political systems of the world were ready, the movie set of the world was ready. The props were in place. The characters were in place. Lights, camera, action!

The time had fully come. The times were ripe. The systems, structures, practices, governments, worldviews, modus operandi, and paradigm shifts had become established. And so "God sent his son, born of a woman, born under law" to inaugurate the times of grace. God sent his son. Jesus was born.

That is why Daniel says that God is the one who orchestrates the times and seasons by setting up or toppling kingdoms to suit his purposes.

When the times were ripe, the divine invaded humanity to enable the human body to house the divine.

When the times were ripe, the royal engaged the commoner to enable commoners to become royals.

When the times were ripe, the immortal entered the mortal to enable mortals to become immortals.

When the times were ripe, the wealthy entered the poor to enable the poor to become wealthy.

When the times were ripe, the imperishable took on the perishable to enable the perishable to become imperishable.

When the times were ripe, the strong penetrated the weak to enable the weak to become strong.

When the times were ripe, the omnipotent wore the impotent to enable the powerless to become powerful.

Allow the Holy Spirit to use you in establishing the times

In the beginning of time, the Spirit of God hovered around the void and became the agent of creation. Then again at the dawn of the times of grace, the Holy Spirit hovered around the chaotic world and became the agent of recreation to establish the times of grace.

The actors God placed to establish the times of grace allowed the Holy Spirit to use them in the act of recreation. That is, they received and exercised the Issachar Anointing. You can also be an actor in the divine calendar by allowing the Holy Spirit to use you in establishing the times. May you open yourself to receive the Issachar Anointing in order to become an actor in establishing the times!

Those Who Ignored the Holy Spirit and Missed the Times

When the times were ripe and God sent his Son, certain important groups missed the times of grace because they were not in tune with the Holy Spirit and ignored the promptings of the Holy Spirit.

The Pharisees missed the signs of the times of grace

The Pharisees missed the signs of the times of grace. They had a reputation as the group that interpreted Mosaic Law accurately and strictly. After Israel's rampant apostasy and punishment through exile, the Pharisees arose as a movement to ensure compliance with God's law. The Pharisees had good intentions, but along the line they lost their main purpose, which was to guide Israel and avoid the consequence of rejection by God.

The Pharisees focused on inessentials and looked at the letter of the law instead of the spirit of the law. They became people who contravened the intentions of the law by developing interpretations that contradicted the spirit of the law. They became more concerned with traditions, external observances, religiosity, and societal respect. Consequently, they were no longer in tune with the Spirit to welcome the arrival of the times of grace. They received no sign of the birth of our Lord Jesus Christ and were upstaged by poor shepherds watching their flocks by night.

Today, we have many Pharisees in our churches. There are people who focus on traditions rather than the Spirit of God. There are people who focus on the form rather than the content, and hence promote external observances rather than true inner purity. There are people who quench the movement of the Holy Spirit by rules developed to maintain decorum in church.

I am not saying this to promote disorderliness. God is the God of order. I am saying that we have a God who moves by his Spirit in unexpected ways and by uncharted methods of operation.

The Pharisees of our time see Christmas as a time for religious observances such as Christmas conventions, Christmas services, Christmas caroling, Advent programs, and so on. These, in and of themselves, are not bad. Sometimes, however, they push aside fellowship with the Holy Spirit and fail to recognize the fact that Christmas marked the dawn of the times of grace. They fail to flow with the times of grace.

May you not be like a Pharisee, but be an agent of the Holy Spirit in establishing the times!

The Sadducees missed the signs of the times of grace

The Sadducees missed the signs of the times of grace. They were aristocratic, priestly, rich families, who had power under Roman rule and from whom high priests were chosen. They were most concerned about their financial and elite social status, and desired to maintain their political clout in the Roman province of Israel. They were not in tune with the Spirit to welcome the arrival of the times of grace. As a result, they received no sign of the birth of our Lord Jesus Christ and were also upstaged by the poor shepherds.

Today, we have Sadducees who are only interested in gaining and maintaining their positions in the church. They play politics and look out for what they can get out of the church. They strive to become pastors so that they can get money from the church members. They punish those who speak the truth about their misdeeds. They push aside the Spirit of God and operate in the flesh. They have become people of this world in this world.

Consequently, the Sadducees of our time see Christmas as a time to adorn their communities, church, and homes with Christmas lights and decorations, a time to receive gifts from members, a time to raise funds for their ministries. In doing so, they often push aside fellowship with the Holy Spirit and fail to flow with the times of grace.

May you not be like a Sadducee but be an agent of the Holy Spirit in establishing the times!

The Sanhedrin missed the signs of the times of grace

The Sanhedrin missed the signs of the times of grace. They were the ruling body of Israel, consisting of Sadducees and Pharisees. They were most concerned about securing their hegemony over the temple and religious life. They were concerned with not doing anything to cause the Roman Empire to remove them from their governing role. That is why they attempted to stop the disciples from preaching the gospel after the day of Pentecost. They were not in tune with the Spirit to welcome the arrival of the times of grace. Even though they correctly interpreted the prophecy of Jesus's birthplace, they failed to go worship the Messiah with the magi.

Today, we have Sanhedrins in the form of church presbytery, church diaconate, church sessions, church councils, and so on who are focused on maintaining their authority over their respective congregations rather than promoting the movement of the Holy Spirit in the church. Some such groups feel threatened by the overt acts of the Holy Spirit in the congregation, and rather than seek to flow with it, they look to stop it. By pushing aside vibrant fellowship with the Holy Spirit, these people fail to flow with the times of grace.

May you not be like a Sanhedrin member but be an agent of the Holy Spirit in establishing the times!

Those Who Allowed the Holy Spirit to Show Them the Times

When the times were ripe and God sent his Son, some people who were in tune with the Holy Spirit received the promptings of the Holy Spirit and welcomed the arrival of the times of grace. These people not only saw the signs but also acted upon the times and became agents of God's orchestration of the times.

The magi saw the signs of and acted upon the times of grace

Consider the following passage: "After Jesus was born in Bethlehem in Judea, during the time of King Herod, Magi from the east came to Jerusalem and asked, 'Where is the one who has been born king of the Jews? We saw his star in the east and have come to worship him'" (Matt. 2:1–2).

The star of the King of the Jews that the magi saw appeared in the sky, available for all to see. But only the magi saw the sign of the incarnation represented by the star.

The magi were not Yahweh worshippers. They are believed to have been Zoroastrian priests who were adept in astrology and interpreting dreams. They were constantly looking for signs in the heavens that reflected changing times on the earth.

If you're searching or researching, then you're likely to make a discovery. If, however, you're not looking for something, then when you stumble upon a discovery, you may not recognize its significance.

I said earlier that the quest for discovery and curiosity about nature's signs is a quality of the Issachar Anointing. The magi were determined to discover signs and understand them, and in that zeal they ended up following the star for hundreds of miles to understand its target. The Holy Spirit opened their eyes. The Holy Spirit used the star to lead them to Bethlehem, to worship the newly incarnated Son of God, the baby Jesus.

May the Holy Spirit open your eyes to see the signs of the times and so become an agent in establishing the times!

Simeon saw the signs of and acted upon the times of grace

Consider the following passage:

> Now there was a man in Jerusalem called Simeon, who was righteous and devout. He was waiting for the consolation of Israel, and the Holy Spirit was upon him. It had been revealed to him by the Holy Spirit that he would not die before he had seen the Lord's Christ. Moved by the Spirit, he went into the temple courts. When the parents brought in the child Jesus to do for him what the custom of the Law required, Simeon took him in his arms and praised God, saying: "Sovereign Lord, as you have promised, you now dismiss your servant in peace. For my eyes have seen your salvation, which you have prepared in the sight of all people, a light for revelation to the Gentiles and for glory to your people Israel." (Luke 2:25–32)

In a big university town, the economy is dependent on the university. In the same way, the Jerusalem economy centered on the temple as an institution. Mosaic Law provided opportunities for business to flourish. The offerings and sacrifices had exact requirements that a worshipper had to meet. People came from all parts of Israel to offer sacrifices; rather than carry their items for the sacrifices, worshippers bought the prescribed items in the courtyards of the temple.

There were sellers of the temple coin, who were known as moneychangers. There were sellers of pigeons and doves, sellers of sheep without blemish, sellers of male or female goats without defect, sellers of flour and grain and salt for the grain offering, and sellers of young bulls without defect. There were wholesalers and retailers and agents who bought on behalf of worshippers. There were agents of innkeepers who advertised their accommodation for travelers who came to offer sacrifices.

Thus the "temple courts," mentioned in verse 27, together became a huge marketplace, the center of the Jerusalem economy. The temple courts were very crowded with the traders, buyers, worshippers, priests, rabbis, and so on. It was as busy an open-air market as Makola Market in Accra, Ghana.

The above text tells us that Simeon was righteous and devout. "Righteous" means that he believed solely in God and had absolute faith in God. "Devout" means that he was God-fearing, devoted to worshipping God, and sincere and earnest in worshipping God. We learn that the Holy Spirit was upon him. This indicates a pervasive presence and not a momentary descending of the Holy Spirit.

We also learn that he was looking for the consolation of Israel. That is, he was praying and waiting for the advent of the Christ who would bring comfort to Israel. Zechariah, the father of John the Baptist, explained that this consolation of Israel meant (1) salvation of Israel from their enemies, (2) protection to worship God without persecution, and (3) the arrival of Christ as the light to shine on those in darkness.[1] Simeon never gave up his role as a lookout for the arrival of the times of Israel's consolation, which I call the times of grace, throughout the many years of his life.

Into the open-air market of the temple courts walks an ordinary-looking couple with an ordinary-looking baby. In fact, Isaiah says about Jesus that "he had no beauty or majesty to attract us to him, nothing in his appearance that we should desire him" (Isa. 53:2). You could deduce that this was not a cute baby. There was nothing that would draw Simeon's attention to this young family.

But as soon as Joseph and Mary entered the temple courts, Simeon was moved by the Holy Spirit to go there too. He was in touch with the Spirit, so he had assurance of the accuracy of his impulse. He made a beeline through the crowds and came up to this ordinary-looking couple with an ordinary-looking baby. Then he made his declaration that the times of grace had dawned: "Sovereign Lord, as you have promised, you now dismiss your servant in peace. For my eyes have seen your salvation, which you have prepared in the sight of all people, a light for revelation to the Gentiles and for glory to your people Israel."

Simeon saw the signs of the times of grace and acted upon them because he was righteous, strong in faith, devout, and filled with the Holy Spirit. He knew to expect the sign and was looking for it.

This is a quality of the Issachar Anointing. Just like the men of Issachar, Simeon understood the times through the Holy Spirit.

Anna saw the signs of and acted upon the times of grace

Consider the following passage: "There was also a prophetess, Anna, the daughter of Phanuel, of the tribe of Asher. She was very old; she had lived with her husband seven years after her marriage, and then was a widow until she was eighty-four. She never left the temple but worshiped night and day, fasting and praying. Coming up to them at that very moment, she gave thanks to God and spoke about the child to all who were looking forward to the redemption of Jerusalem" (Luke 2:36–38).

This passage tells us that the prophetess Anna was an eighty-four-year-old widow who kept herself pure. She never departed from the temple—that is, from the sight of God. She worshipped, fasted, and prayed day and night; she consistently practiced the spiritual disciplines.

In the same temple courts, Anna also made a beeline through the crowds and came up to this ordinary-looking couple with an ordinary-looking baby. She also took the baby Jesus and proclaimed to all that this was the Redeemer of the world. In the hustle and bustle of the temple market, Anna was able to see from afar and know that the sign of the times was in the crowds.

Anna saw the sign of the times of grace and acted on it because she was pure, stayed in the presence of God, and practiced the spiritual disciplines. Consequently, she had revelations from God through the Spirit and ended up heralding the dawn of the times of grace.

Summary

When the times were ripe and God sent his Son, certain important groups missed the times of grace because they were not in tune with the Holy Spirit and ignored the promptings of the Holy Spirit.

There were some people, however, who were in tune with the Holy Spirit and so received the promptings of the Holy Spirit. They became agents in establishing the times of grace, and welcomed the arrival of the times of grace.

The magi had a habit of studying the skies for revelation and symbolism. In so doing, they received the Holy Spirit's revelation of the emerging times. May you seek to understand the times through the Holy Spirit!

Zechariah, Mary, and Joseph saw the signs of and acted upon the times because of their faith. May God strengthen your faith in order to understand the times!

Simeon saw the signs of and acted upon the times because (1) he was filled with the Holy Spirit; (2) he had revelation of the advent of Christ; (3) he waited upon

God in prayer, looking for Christ's advent; and (4) he allowed the Holy Spirit to lead him to Christ.

Anna saw the signs of and acted upon the times because (1) she worshipped daily, (2) she waited upon God in prayer and fasting, and (3) she allowed the Holy Spirit to lead her to Christ.

The Holy Spirit will reveal the times and seasons to you if you truly accept Jesus Christ as your personal Savior and Lord in total surrender, and practice the following spiritual disciplines:

- Wait upon God in prayer and fasting.
- Spend personal time in true worship.
- Strengthen your faith in biblical revelation.
- Ask for the daily infilling of the Holy Spirit.
- Ask for the Holy Spirit to reveal to you the significance of signs and events in nature and world affairs.

May God open your eyes to see the power of the Holy Spirit for giving you the Issachar Anointing for understanding the times and impacting your generation!

5

Acquiring Issachar Anointing through Spiritual Formation

Daniel was a person who gained an Issachar-type anointing for understanding the times through spiritual formation.

> Then the king ordered Ashpenaz, chief of his court officials, to bring in some of the Israelites from the royal family and the nobility—young men without any physical defect, handsome, showing aptitude for every kind of learning, well informed, quick to understand, and qualified to serve in the king's palace. He was to teach them the language and literature of the Babylonians. The king assigned them a daily amount of food and wine from the king's table. They were to be trained for three years, and after that they were to enter the king's service.

> Among these were some from Judah: Daniel, Hananiah, Mishael and Azariah. The chief official gave them new names: to Daniel, the name Belteshazzar; to Hananiah, Shadrach; to Mishael, Meshach; and to Azariah, Abednego.
>
> But Daniel resolved not to defile himself with the royal food and wine, and he asked the chief official for permission not to defile himself this way. (Dan. 1:3–8)

When we think of the book of Daniel, we fondly remember the mighty spiritual exploits of Daniel and his three friends, Shadrach, Meshach, and Abednego, who were living as aliens in a foreign land, Babylonia. We remember how, in chapter 2, God miraculously revealed Nebuchadnezzar's dream to Daniel, and how God miraculously enabled Daniel to interpret the dream so that Nebuchadnezzar spared all the wise men, including Daniel and his friends, from death. We also remember the account in chapter 3 of Shadrach, Meshach, and Abednego, who refused to bow to the golden image and were sentenced to death by burning in a fiery oven, and how God miraculously delivered them from that sentence. We also remember the account in chapter 6 of Daniel, who refused to pray to King Darius, but continued to pray to God. He was sentenced to death in a lions' den, and God miraculously delivered him from that death.

When we hear these accounts, we are encouraged about the power and faithfulness of God to deliver us from trials. But seldom do we examine what enabled these four Jewish youths, aliens in a foreign land, to accomplish the mighty spiritual exploits that gave them great success in their careers. What was different about these four boys? What enabled them to stand boldly for God in the face of imminent death when other Jews abandoned God?

What was different was that they focused on spiritual formation through the practice of spiritual disciplines. Their practice enabled them to understand the times. If you are going to live a victorious Christian life, then you must practice spiritual disciplines for spiritual formation in order to gain understanding of the times.

Mighty Exploits of Daniel and Friends Were Rooted in Pursuit of Holiness

In those days, Babylonia was a modern nation with advanced learning, magnificent buildings, comprehensive infrastructure, strong economy, and comfortable life. Babylonia's stature was similar to that of the United States today. The four Jewish boys were among the lucky exiles from Judah, because they were placed in the king's palace to be trained as government officers. Remember that a few months earlier, they had been living in the midst of turmoil in the hell called Judah. Life had become increasingly oppressive with siege after siege, famine after famine, and war after war. Then, suddenly, they found themselves living in the palace of the most powerful kingdom on earth, not as servants but as nobles.

When they arrived in Babylon, Daniel and his friends were placed in the royal academy to be trained to become government leaders. They were required to eat royal food, which was sumptuously prepared with all kinds of meats and the best wines. "Daniel resolved not to defile himself with the royal food and wine, and he asked the chief official for permission not to defile himself this way." Daniel saw that the royal food broke Levitical dietary laws and would defile them. The four youths resolved to keep on keeping the faith. They decided that in spite of all the luxury and prestige, they would not defile themselves with the worldly values of Babylon. They would remain faithful to Yahweh. They would remember Yahweh's faithfulness to them in Judah during their troubles. They would remember their God, who always remembered them during their trials. They would keep on keeping the faith.

Daniel had Issachar Anointing that Facilitates Understanding of the Times

Daniel's worldview had been shaped in the palace in Judah and in the temple in Jerusalem through study of the Bible. He was intelligent and learned according to Daniel 1:4. Later on in the book of Daniel, we discover that Daniel was an expert in the Bible. He was very faithful to God in refusing to pray to King Darius. He believed God would deliver him from the lions' den. He had revelations from God; God showed Nebuchadnezzar's dream to him, as well as the end times after his twenty-one-day fast. Daniel was prayerful; his jealous colleagues perceived that forbidding prayer was the only way to trap him into breaking contrived Babylonian law. He fasted frequently, as documented in many accounts of Daniel waiting upon God for revelation, understanding, and favor. The angel Gabriel said Daniel was highly esteemed (Dan. 9:23).

Based on the forgoing qualities, we can say that Daniel had an Issachar type of anointing. These are the qualities that facilitate understanding of the times, according to our earlier discussion.

Daniel and Friends Were Blessed because of Their Issachar Anointing

Daniel acted on his resolve and asked the royal official and the guard to excuse him and his three friends from the royal meals. After some hesitation, the royal guard agreed to a science experiment proposed by Daniel concerning the food. Daniel said, "Please test your servants for ten days: Give us nothing but vegetables to eat and water to drink. Then compare our appearance with that of the young men who eat the royal food, and treat your servants in accordance with what you see" (Dan. 1:12–13).

As you may know, in a science experiment there is a control group and an experimental group. In this case the experimental group was Daniel and his friends, who were on a vegetarian diet and drank water. The control group was the rest of the royal academy, who ate normal royal meals. Both groups were examined after ten days to see who had better appearance. This is one of the first recorded uses of what we call today the modern scientific method.

"At the end of the ten days they [Daniel, Shadrach, Meshach, and Abednego] looked healthier and better nourished than any of the young men who ate the royal food. So the guard took away their choice food and the wine they were to drink and gave them vegetables instead" (Dan. 1:15-16).

In this way, Daniel and his friends continued their royal training without defiling themselves and kept their faith intact. "To these four young men God gave knowledge and understanding of all kinds of literature and learning. And Daniel could understand visions and dreams of all kinds ... In every matter of wisdom and understanding about which the king questioned them, he found them ten times better than all the magicians and enchanters in his whole kingdom" (Dan. 1:17, 20).

God made Daniel and his friends healthier and gave them wisdom, knowledge, and understanding. The four of them placed at the top of the royal academy's graduating class, far above any graduating class ever.

This wisdom, knowledge, and understanding that God gave them were Issachar Anointing qualities that enabled them to understand the times. God enabled Daniel and his friends to do mighty exploits and become successful to the point that Daniel was named the prime minister of Babylon.

Spiritual Formation for the Issachar Anointing

Daniel's advanced spiritual formation enabled him to develop Issachar-type anointing. The following spiritual disciplines will help you to obtain the spiritual formation needed for the Issachar Anointing:

1. Study the Bible thoroughly and apply biblical principles to your life.
2. Seek incarnation of biblical insights and revelations in your life.
3. Develop a biblical worldview by viewing events and occurrences through the lens of the Bible. This means frequent Bible study so that biblical thoughts and ideas become part of your thought process and conscience.
4. Pray for wisdom because wisdom belongs to God.
5. Resolve not to defile yourself with worldly ways. God is holy, and you must be holy to receive from him.
6. Let the Holy Spirit minister to you and take heed of his promptings.
7. Spend time in private worship and meditation. Enter the presence and glory of God. Listen to God's voice, reflect on his might and grace, recall his actions, and review his commands. Open your soul for God to tangibly inhabit you.

6

Leveraging the Issachar Anointing to Change the Times and Seasons

The times of the great recession in the United States spanned the years 2007 through 2010, during which time most economies in the world also experienced negative growth. During those times, it was difficult to find jobs, and the few jobs available did not pay well. Benefits were cut and people took multiple, low-paying, part-time jobs to replace the well-paid full-time jobs they had lost. No matter how hard he or she tried, the average person could not be successful in the times of the great recession. The times of the great recession were not conducive to professional and financial success in general.

The times have a significant impact on your progress and well-being in life. So, when the times are bad, you need someone to change the times. It is not so much that you must change to become successful, but that the times must change to become more conducive to your success.

God Orchestrates Times and Seasons

When Daniel prayed that God would tell him Nebuchadnezzar's dream and its interpretation, God answered his prayer. In a thanksgiving for answered prayers, Daniel revealed several characteristics of God: "He changes times and seasons; he sets up kings and deposes them. He gives wisdom to the wise and knowledge to the discerning" (Dan. 2:21).

Scientific research has shown that a good conductor can conduct an orchestra to produce great sound. A bad conductor can conduct the same orchestra playing the same music and produce inferior sound.[1] The conductor affects the way the orchestra plays together because she or he directs when each instrument comes in, for how long, and how intensely. The conductor controls how the various parts blend together. So we say the conductor is the orchestrator of the music.

According to Daniel 2:21, God is the orchestrator of the times and seasons. The players that characterize a given time or season are placed in those roles by God. As part of changing times and seasons, God may also change those players. God is in control of everything. He gives wisdom and knowledge to his children to operate within the times and seasons, whether these are times of trouble or progress, seasons of drought or fruitfulness.

No matter what the time or season, God can change them. God can change the them because the whole world is in his hands. Just as you hold a globe in your hands, so God holds the world in his hands. He possesses the power to control everything that happens in the world.

Like a conductor, God orchestrates all events, weather systems, natural phenomenon, and every other aspect of the operation of the world, in fulfillment of his purposes.

God can change the times and seasons because he is the omnipotent God and nothing can disrupt his plans. He is immutable, the God who never changes. When the times or seasons change, he remains the same! When the times or seasons are troubled, he does not change. When the times or seasons are good, he does not change. He remains the same yesterday, today, and forever.

Leverage the Issachar Anointing to Change the Times and Seasons

After you use the Issachar Anointing to understand the times and seasons, you may conclude that the times or seasons do not favor you or your organization. In fact, they may be inimical to your well-being or your organization's well-being. It will be helpful, therefore, if the times and seasons can be changed in your favor. Since God is the one who controls the times and seasons, you must go to God and ask him for change.

Intel Corporation is the largest manufacturer of the key central processing unit (CPU) chip used in PC-style computers. To distinguish its chip from those of other manufacturers, Intel has created a label that is affixed to computers containing its premier CPU. The label says, "Intel Inside," which means the computer is Intel powered.

As we discussed earlier, the Holy Spirit is at the heart of the Issachar Anointing. Taking a page out of Intel's marketing, we can say that the Issachar Anointing implies "Holy Spirit Inside," which means the Issachar Anointing is Holy Spirit powered. The Holy Spirit, who is God, is also the only one who can change the times or seasons. This means that you can leverage the Holy Spirit powered Issachar Anointing to change the times or seasons.

The Issachar Anointing is like a lever in science. A lever is "a rigid bar resting on a pivot, used to help move a heavy or firmly fixed load with one end when pressure is applied to the other."[2] A lever "can be used to exert a large force over a small distance at one end by exerting only a small force over a greater distance at the other."[3]

R. A. Torrey said, "Prayer can do anything that God can do, and as God can do anything, prayer is omnipotent."[4] Prayer can move the hand of God. When you acquire the Holy Spirit powered Issachar Anointing, it becomes a lever that you may use to move the hand of God to change the times or seasons.

God is sovereign. He can change the times and seasons to suit his purposes whenever he wants. In his sovereignty, however, God has asked his children to pray to him about their needs. Scripture is replete with examples of God's answer to prayer. So it is proper to ask God to change the times and seasons when they don't favor you.

The Issachar Anointing positions you to press such a request to God. In the larger scheme of things, exercising your Issachar Anointing is relatively small compared to the change in the times and seasons that God will effect. An exercise of your Issachar Anointing is small, but it effects God's changes in the times and seasons, which are large. Small begets large, which is the definition of leverage. This is why I refer to praying for change as leveraging the Issachar Anointing to change the times and seasons.

Leverage the Holy Spirit powered Issachar Anointing to change times of trouble into times of progress. Leverage the Issachar Anointing to change your season of drought into a season of fruitfulness.

May God depose leaders who have cultivated times of trouble or seasons of drought, and install leaders to usher in and sustain times of progress and seasons of fruitfulness!

Daniel's Times and Seasons Prompted His Observation

Daniel lived through several times and seasons and so was qualified to observe that God is the orchestrator of times and seasons.

Daniel lived in times of trouble and hardship in Judah. Life became increasingly oppressive with siege after siege, famine after famine, and war after war, culminating in the conquest of Judah. After the conquest of Judah, he lived in times of captivity, becoming a prisoner of war exiled to Babylon.

During the times of captivity, God smiled upon him and gave him a season of fruitfulness. He was chosen to attend the royal academy for training to become a Babylonian government official. Upon graduation, he was appointed royal counselor.

Then Daniel entered a season of trouble when Nebuchadnezzar threatened to kill all the royal counselors unless they told him his dream and interpreted it.

Daniel, knowing that God is the one who changes times and seasons, prayed to God about his season of trouble. In response to Daniel's prayer, God changed his season of trouble into a season of fruitfulness: he gave Daniel the dream and its interpretation. Daniel was promoted to prime minister of Babylon and entered into a new season of fruitfulness. In a sense, he leveraged the Holy Spirit powered Issachar Anointing.

While Daniel was still in times of captivity, his Babylonian coworkers, out of jealousy, caused King Darius to issue an edict requiring everyone to pray only to him. Daniel violated this edict and found himself in another season of trouble as he was thrown into the lions' den.

Though it is not recorded I believe that Daniel prayed for God to change this season of trouble. God came through for Daniel once again and shut the mouths of the lions. When King Darius realized that God had protected Daniel from the lions, he released him from the lions' den. Daniel was restored to his position and entered another season of fruitfulness. God enhanced this season by causing King Darius to throw Daniel's enemies into the lions' den, where they were promptly killed by the lions. You see, God deposed those jealous royal officials in order to create a new season of fruitfulness for Daniel.

There are many other examples, but these times and seasons in Daniel's life enable us to understand why he made the observation about God's unique role as the orchestrator of times and seasons.

So the times and seasons have significant impacts on your progress in life. When the times or seasons are bad, therefore, you need to leverage the Issachar Anointing to change the times or seasons.

The Times in the World

The times affect your progress in life

The times are the thinking, worldview, occurrences, and situations that characterize a period in a given geographical grouping and/or sociocultural/religious grouping. That is, the times are the general conditions of the world globally and the situation around you. The times can affect your progress in life. When a nation's economy is good, your chances of prosperity are high. Otherwise, no matter how hard you work, you will struggle to make ends meet. For example, in the 1960s, university graduates in Ghana were automatically guaranteed prosperity because of the times. The times in Ghana today make it extremely difficult for university graduates to even get jobs.

There's a story in from the group Humans of New York, posted on Instagram on December 8, 2015, about a scientist and inventor who lived in Syria. Before the war, he was prosperous and successful. In times of peace, he was successful because of his profession and business acumen. After the war started, he lost everything and could not practice his science. He fled to Istanbul, Turkey, where Syrians live as refugees. He entered times of refugee status. He could not get a job at a university, even though he was known as an accomplished scientist and they used a book he wrote as a textbook.

You can be accomplished, with great expertise in your profession, but when you live in times of trouble, it will be difficult, if not impossible, for you to succeed.

Please note that not all failures or difficulties are because of the times. Sometimes you cause your own problems. In some instances, however, the times just don't favor you. You need more favorable times in order to succeed. That is why, when you are in times of trouble, you have to leverage the Issachar Anointing to change the times.

To make ends meet, this Syrian scientist created architectural designs. Turkish citizens paid him 1 percent of the normal price for them, and in turn sold them for high prices because, as a noncitizen, he could not present his designs himself for full compensation. He said, "There is no respect of my work here [in Turkey]." His life in war-torn Syria and then Turkey was what I call life in times of turmoil. The conditions of the world around him were not conducive to thriving. No matter how hard he worked in times of turmoil, he could not be successful. To be successful, he had to wait for new times of progress.

By the grace of God, this Syrian man has moved to Troy, Michigan, where he plans to continue his research and invention work to become successful. His arrival in Troy marked a transition into times of progress. The general conditions around him are conducive to success.

God can change the times miraculously

Ecclesiastes 3:1 says, "There is a time for everything, and a season for every activity under heaven." No matter your troubles, only God can change the times that foment those troubles. God can depose kings and officials who cultivate times of trouble and install new kings or officials to usher in times of progress. He will give you wisdom and knowledge to operate in the new times.

God can change the times miraculously within a very short span of time. Sometimes when you understand how a certain system works, it is difficult to see how matters can change without going through the normal process of the system. For example, there are certain principles that apply to an economy. One such principle is the law of supply and demand. When there is scarcity of supply of a given commodity and overabundance of demand, then the price for the commodity is going to be extremely high. This is because many people are trying to buy a scarce commodity, and the tendency for the sellers is to raise the price. Conversely, when there is overabundance of supply and few buyers, the price goes down. Buyers have more bargaining power, and sellers have to lower their prices to compete for the few buyers.

We've seen this law of supply and demand operating in the oil market. A few years ago, oil was selling for more than one hundred dollars a barrel. At the time of this writing, the oil supply has increased a lot and the Chinese economy has faltered, so their demand for oil has gone down. Consequently, the world has overabundant supply of oil and lower demand. This has plunged the price for oil to an average of thirty-five dollars a barrel.

Supply and demand is a well-accepted and proven principle of economics. When you know this economic principle, it is difficult to see how an economy can bypass this principle and change overnight.

God can, however, change the times in an economy miraculously within a short time, in spite of or even because of the principles of economics. The Bible records one such example in 2 Kings 6–7, when God changed times of trouble and hardship in Israel to times of peace and prosperity in less than twenty-four hours!

The siege of Samaria by Aram caused unimaginable famine. Israel practiced cannibalism and ate unclean animals:

> As the king of Israel was passing by on the wall, a woman cried to him, "Help me, my lord the king!"
>
> The king replied, "If the Lord does not help you, where can I get help for you? From the threshing floor? From the winepress?" Then he asked her, "What's the matter?"

> She answered, "This woman said to me, 'Give up your son so we may eat him today, and tomorrow we'll eat my son.' So we cooked my son and ate him. The next day I said to her, 'Give up your son so we may eat him,' but she had hidden him." (2 Kings 6:26–29)

Those were times of trouble and hardship. The king of Israel and his army chief reluctantly consulted Elisha about this grave situation. Elisha prophesied that the famine would end within twenty-four hours: "Hear the word of the LORD. This is what the LORD says: About this time tomorrow, a seah of flour will sell for a shekel and two seahs of barley for a shekel at the gate of Samaria" (2 Kings 7:1).

It seemed impossible that prices could tumble that fast. According to the economic principle of supply and demand, prices of commodities were high because there was negligible supply and extremely high demand. According to human understanding, supply could not increase overnight to dramatically bring down prices and immediately improve the economy. Even if the Arameans withdrew their siege and the people planted crops, it would take months to increase supply.

These economic facts were likely on the mind of the army chief. He clearly found Elisha's prophecy nonsensical. He ridiculed Elisha, saying, "Look, even if the LORD should open the floodgates of the heavens, could this happen?" (2 Kings 7:2).

Elisha further prophesied that the army chief would see the times of peace and prosperity but not enjoy them. Elisha understood human economics, but he was operating on divine economics. Elisha knew that God had the power to change the times, using any method that he desired. God could operate within human economics, or he could circumvent them for his own purposes.

At nightfall that same day, some lepers at the city gate risked death and entered the camp of the Arameans. The lepers found out that the Arameans had fled the camp. The Lord had driven them away with sounds of approaching chariots, horses, and soldiers.

God can use anyone to bring change in the times, because "he sets up kings and deposes them" in order to establish the times that he desires. So don't belittle yourself. Be an instrument for God to use to change the times. Know that God can change the times, and leverage the Issachar Anointing to bring change to the times.

After eating to their fill, the lepers reported their discovery to the city gatekeeper, who reported it to the king. After further investigation, the king allowed the people of Samaria to enter the deserted Aramean camp, and they collected enough food and supplies. God had miraculously increased supply. It now far exceeded the number of people in Samaria. The prices of commodities dropped dramatically. This had an immediate ripple effect throughout the economy and brought immediate prosperity to Samaria.

The people's rush to the Aramean camp caused a stampede that killed the army chief. God had miraculously changed the times of trouble and hardship into times of peace and prosperity, but the army chief did not enjoy the new times because of his attitude toward the man of God.

Though it is not recorded, I believe that Elisha prayed to leverage the Issachar Anointing to change the times.

God truly "changes times and seasons; he sets up kings and deposes them." So, leverage the Issachar Anointing to change the times to favor your progress! Ask God to depose leaders who have cultivated times of trouble and install leaders to usher in and sustain times of progress!

The Seasons of Life within the Times

The times may be generally favorable, but you may be in a season of drought. As I said earlier, there are seasons within times. A season is characterized by the general conditions governing your life in a given location. Seasons can be in different aspects of your life, such as marriage, family, spirituality, ministry, career, finances, education, and health.

A plant needs the right season before it can flourish

A biome consists of the climate, terrain, geology, soils, and vegetation that support particular plants and animals. A season is a time period during which there is a particular combination of weather and environment in a given biome.

A season that is characterized by hard or infertile soil and drought in the biome may be suitable for a given plant but deadly for another plant. A season that is characterized by floods may be suitable for a given plant but deadly for another plant. If the plant is not in the right season, it will die no matter how well you take care of it.

For example, a plantain tree will not survive in Massachusetts because it needs a warm dry season and a warm rainy season within a tropical forest biome. Similarly, an apple tree will not survive in Ghana because it needs winter, spring, summer, and autumn within a temperate deciduous forest biome. No matter how well you take care of these plants, they will not survive in the wrong biome. If you want them to survive, you have to change the biome and hence the seasons.

You need the right season in the right location before you can flourish

Similarly, everyone has a season, which is the general condition governing your life in a given location. The season you find yourself in affects your progress and well-being.

Your season is dependent on your location. You have to be in the right location to experience seasons that are beneficial. If you're in the wrong location, then even in times of progress, you will not experience the seasons that you need to be successful.

Many years ago, we met a lawyer from Ghana who was trying to get into the legal profession in the

United States. The American economy was good, but she was not doing well. She finally decided to change locations and returned to Ghana, where she became a top corporate lawyer. Though the United States was in times of progress, the location was wrong for her, plunging her into a season of drought until she changed locations. Then she entered a season of fruitfulness.

If you're in the right location, then even in times of trouble you can experience the seasons that will favor your success. When Daniel was in the times of captivity in Babylon, his location in the palace was conducive for him to experience seasons of fruitfulness.

For God to change your season, he may have to change your location.

I had a season of drought once when another company acquired the company I worked for. The executives of the new company were hostile to progressive management principles and cultivated an atmosphere of fear and intimidation. These conditions were not conducive to engineering creativity. In this season of drought, no matter how hard I worked I was not successful. I was in the wrong season by virtue of the wrong location. What I needed was not necessarily to work harder, but to change my season and/or location.

Not long after I started working there, I was fired in a spectacular fashion, along with three colleagues. I did not prosper at that company, and it was a stifling experience for me.

After leaving that company, I joined another company that ushered me into a season of progress and success. God used my firing to remove me from the wrong location. He terminated my season of drought and took me to a new location that ushered me into a season of progress and success. God, effectively, removed me from an environment where the executives cultivated my season of drought.

The passage "God sets up kings and deposes them" applies to leaders of any organization. God can change your current season by either installing new leaders or deposing existing leaders. God can change your current season by allowing you to be laid off or be pushed to resign. Then he'll bring you into a new organization that will foster a new season of fruitfulness. So, when the times are good but you're in a season of drought in a given organization, you should pray for God to change your organization to give you seasons of fruitfulness.

May God change your location and environment and give you a season of fruitfulness!

Only God can change your season to a fruitful season

No matter your situation, only God can change your season. God can depose kings and officials that cultivate your season of drought and install new kings or officials to usher in your season of fruitfulness. He will give you wisdom and knowledge to operate in your new season. So leverage the Issachar Anointing to change your season to favor your progress!

We encountered a student who was afflicted by disease that caused her not to be able to focus on her academic work. She was not doing well in the university, though she was very smart. She was in a season of sickness and failure, even though she lived in the United States in times of progress.

We took her through deliverance prayers during an all-night prayer session, and she was delivered of demonic possession. The disease left her, and she was able to study and successfully graduated from the university. When God came into the situation, he changed her season of sickness and failure into a season of health and success. We leveraged the Holy Spirit-powered Issachar Anointing to change her season.

Leverage the Issachar Anointing to change your season to favor your progress!

May God depose demonic powers that have cultivated your season of trouble!

May God install divine powers to usher in and sustain your season of progress!

Summary

The times and seasons have a significant impact on your progress in life or your organization's progress. When the times or seasons are bad, you need someone to change them. Only God can change the times or seasons.

You should leverage the Issachar Anointing to change the times of trouble into times of progress. You should leverage the Issachar Anointing to change your season of drought into a season of fruitfulness.

> I pray that the eyes of your heart may be enlightened in order that you may know the hope to which he has called you, the riches of his glorious inheritance in the saints, and his incomparably great power for us who believe. That power is like the working of his mighty strength, which he exerted in Christ when he raised him from the dead and seated him at his right hand in the heavenly realms, far above all rule and authority, power and dominion, and every title that can be given, not only in the present age but also in the one to come. (Eph. 1:18–21)

Amen!

7

Bible Study

This Bible Study chapter is meant to assist you to further explore how to apply the framework for understanding the times covered in this book. The study will explore the role of the Holy Spirit as part of the framework, the cause and consequences for failing to understand the times, and application of the framework to your personal life.

Failure to Understand the Times: King Rehoboam

Rehoboam failed to understand the times

Read I Kings 11:28–31, 26, 40.
Read 1 Kings 12:1–15.

Define the times by answering these questions:

1. What transition was taking place in this episode?
2. What are the occurrences in this episode?

3. What are the prevailing thoughts expressed in this episode and by which parties?
4. What situation(s) characterized the transition?
5. What geographical area is covered by this episode?
6. What systems and structures were under pressure for change during the transition?
7. Are there any spiritual underpinnings of the Times?
8. What key element(s) for Understanding the Times did Rehoboam fail to employ to Understand the Times?

Rehoboam lost northern tribes for failing to understand the times

Read 1 Kings 12:16–20.

1. What were the consequences of failure to understand the times?
2. What lessons have you learned to apply to your life?

Summary

Wisdom is an essential element of the Issachar Anointing needed for understanding the times. Rehoboam failed to ask God for wisdom, as his father Solomon had done. His arrogance and lack of discernment caused him to miss the signs of the times surrounding his ascension to the throne. He paid dearly for this mistake.

Understanding the Times in Your Life Today

Agent for understanding the times

Read Daniel 2:19–23.

1. Who sets up times and seasons?
2. Who gives revelation of the times and seasons?
3. How is this person able to set up times and seasons?
4. How do you acquire understanding of the times and seasons?
5. What skill enables you to understand the times and seasons?

The times in your life

1. Imagine removing yourself from your situation and do the following:
    1.1. Are there any abnormal events in your current life?
    1.2. What assumptions underlie your current life? Are they valid?
    1.3. What are your ideas about the workings in your life?

1.4. What beliefs and traditions have you taken for granted? Do they have biblical basis?

1.5. Have peer pressure or family pressure shaped some viewpoints of your life that are inconsistent with biblical principles?

2. Seek biblical insight into situations and events that are in your life.

3. Meditate on your life and God's superintendence of your life, looking for some providential incidents. Ask God to give you insight into the times that you're in.

Summary

Understanding of the times requires you to acquire the Issachar Anointing through spiritual formation and by applying the Issachar Anointing principles, which include seeking biblical insights, applying a biblical worldview, waiting on the Lord for uncommon revelation, being observant of abnormal events, and challenging prevailing dogma.

Notes

Chapter 1
1. Roger Burlingame, *Henry Ford: A Great Life in Brief* (New York: Alfred Knopf, 1954), 62.
2. Lily Rothman, "The founding of America? It's all about us," *Time*, October 26, 2015, 54.

Chapter 2
1. "Issachar, Tribe of," accessed October 15, 2015, http://www.jewishencyclopedia.com/articles/8335-issachar-tribe-of.
2. Midrash Numbers Rabba, 108 (from sacredtexts.com, Midrash Numbers Rabba is a commentary on the Book of Numbers of the Bible. References to texts within the commentary use page numbers as shown in this footnote)
3. Bromiley, Geoffrey W. (ed). *The International Standard Bible Encyclopedia.* E-text version, 2002: HeavenWord, Inc. Accessed in OliveTree Bible Software
4. "Issachar, Tribe of," accessed October 15, 2015, http://www.jewishencyclopedia.com/articles/8335-issachar-tribe-of: "The Midrash finds in the details of the offering various allusions to the Torah (Num. R. xiii. 15). The tribe of Issachar advised the others to bring six covered wagons and twelve oxen (Num. vii. 3) on which to load the parts of the Tabernacle (Num. R. xii. 19)."

⁵ "Issachar, Tribe of," accessed October 15, 2015, http://www.jewishencyclopedia.com/articles/8335-issachar-tribe-of.

⁶ Gene Bellinger, Durval Castro, and Anthony Mills, "Data, Information, Knowledge, and Wisdom," accessed March 31, 2016, http://www.systems-thinking.org/dikw/dikw.htm.

⁷ See Romans 12:8.

⁸ See 1 Corinthians 12:28.

Chapter 3

¹ Ronald A. Heifetz and Marty Linsky, *Leadership on the Line: Staying Alive through the Dangers of Leading* (Boston: Harvard Business School Press, 2002), 53-54.

Chapter 4

¹ See Luke 1:73, 74–75, 78–79.

Chapter 6

¹ "Do Orchestras Really Need Conductors?" accessed January 18, 2016, http://www.npr.org/sections/deceptivecadence/2012/11/27/165677915/do-orchestras-really-need-conductors.

² Oxford English Dictionary, accessed on 1/27/2016, http://www.oxforddictionaries.com/us/definition/american_english/lever

³ Wikipedia, accessed on 1/27/2016, https://en.wikipedia.org/wiki/Lever

⁴ R. A. Torrey, *The Power of Prayer and the Prayer of Power* (Grand Rapids, MI: Zondervan, 1971), 17.

CPSIA information can be obtained
at www.ICGtesting.com
Printed in the USA
FFHW021246220119
50272002-55278FF